Transparency

Kay Gardiner and Ann Shayne

INTRODUCTION

TRANSPARENCY IS NOT THE FIRST WORD that comes to mind when we think of knitting. Knitting is mostly about covering things up, not revealing them—the thickness of curling cables, the layers of floats that lie stranded behind a Fair Isle yoke—all with the goal of bundling our loved ones and ourselves in woolly cocoons.

But then there's lace, the exception that proves the rule. Take a thin enough thread, work it on big enough needles, and knitting becomes as see-through as a pair of fishnet stockings.

For this Field Guide, we invited Amy Christoffers, one of the most agile designers we know, to explore the idea of transparency. We encouraged her to think beyond the obvious transparency of lace knitting and venture into other ways that transparency is manifested. The projects in this little book are Amy's graceful response to our invitation.

An airy shawl with "windows" of color that form effortlessly, using a technique we think of as "intarsia light," because there's no danger of holes.

A baby sweater (because who meets the world with more honesty and transparency than a baby?) with just a touch of lace and an unusual yet plainly apparent construction.

A cowl that layers lace in a way that both reveals and obscures the pattern, and is an amusingly tricky knit.

A lightweight tee in a fabric that is striped, yet uses only one color of yarn.

As we've watched these projects take shape, we've wanted to knit every one. It's an occupational hazard of working with someone as gifted as Amy Christoffers, and one we are very happy to face.

Kay Ann

COCKLESHELL CARDIGAN

Design by

Amy Christoffers

BABIES ARE THE ULTIMATE IN TRANSPARENCY. Their giant baby eyes gaze upon us with such trust and open curiosity that we cannot help but make piles of handknits for them. We are weak under their adorable spell.

We humbly submit that this cardigan is worthy of every lovely baby. And we are pretty certain that the inventive construction of this cardigan will somehow provide babies an excellent case study in how to be clever. (Start 'em young! The structural engineers of tomorrow need baby cardigans today.)

The two pieces are each cast on at the cuff, then knit all the way to the center of the back. A beautiful bind off up the back marries the simple lace patterns, and voilà: it's a cardigan!

The yarn here, Nutmeg Fibers Hearth, strikes us as maybe the most gentle possible material for swaddling a baby in love. It's merino. Hand-dyed using only natural dyes. The chubby worsted weight means that you can easily knit one up as a baby shower gift in a few days. Only you will know how easy—and fun—it was to make.

KNITTED MEASUREMENTS

Chest: 22 (24, 26, 28)" [56 (61, 66, 71) cm]

Length: 8¼ (10, 11¾, 13½)" [21 (25.5, 30, 34.5) cm] from shoulder

SIZES

0–6 (6–12, 12–18, 18–24) months

MATERIALS

— Hearth by Nutmeg Fibers [100 g skeins, each approx 150 yds (137 m), 100% merino]: 2 (2, 3, 3) skein(s) Flamingo, Light Lac & Iron, Osage & Iron, Udo, Ice, Madder Root, or Rust

— Size US 10 (6 mm) circular needle, 24" (60 cm) long or longer, or size needed to achieve gauge

— Spare size US 10 (6 mm) needle, for 3-Needle BO

— Crochet hook size US H-8 (5 mm), for Front Ties

GAUGE

13 sts and 19 rows = 4" (10 cm) over Rev St st

NOTES

Cardi worked in 2 pieces from cuff to center, then joined at center back using 3-Needle BO. Use circ needle to accommodate large number of sts; do not join.

STITCH PATTERNS

1×1 RIB

(odd number of sts)

— *Row 1 (WS):* P1, *k1, p1; rep from * to end.

— *Row 2:* K1, *p1, k1; rep from * to end.

— Rep Rows 1 and 2 for 1×1 Rib.

SLEEVE PATTERN

[panel of 19 (23, 27, 31) sts] (see chart)

— *Row 1 (RS):* P3, *k1, p1; rep from * to last 2 sts, p2.

— *Row 2 and all WS Rows:* Knit the knit sts and purl the purl sts as they face you.

— *Row 3:* P5, *k1, p1; rep from * to last 4 sts, p4.

— *Row 5:* P7, *k1, p1; rep from * to last 6 sts, p6.

— *Row 7:* P9, *k1, p1; rep from * to last 8 sts, p8.

— *Row 9:* P11, *k1, p1; rep from * to last 10 sts, p10.

— *Row 11:* P13, *k1, p1; rep from * to last 12 sts, p12.

— *Row 13:* P15, *k1, p1; rep from * to last 14 sts, p14.

— *Row 14:* Rep Row 2.

EDGING PATTERN

(multiple of 12 sts + 5) (see chart)

- *Row 1 (RS):* K1, p1, *yo, p2tog, p10; rep from * to last 3 sts, yo, p2tog, k1.
- *Row 2 and all WS Rows:* Knit the knit sts and purl the purl sts as they face you; purl all yos.
- *Row 3:* K1, p1, *k1, p1, yo, p2tog, p6, yo, p2tog; rep from * to last 3 sts, k1, p1, k1.
- *Row 5:* K1, p1, *[k1, p1] twice, yo, p2tog, p2, yo, p2tog, k1, p1; rep from * to last 3 sts, k1, p1, k1.
- *Row 7:* K1, p1, *[k1, p1] 3 times, yo, p2tog, [k1, p1] twice; rep from * to last 3 sts, k1, p1, k1.
- *Rows 9 and 11:* Rep Row 2.
- *Row 12:* Rep Row 2.

RIGHT SIDE

SLEEVE

CO 21 (25, 29, 33) sts. Work in 1×1 Rib for 5 rows.

- *Next Row (RS):* K1, work Sleeve Pattern (beg and end where indicated for size if working from chart) to last st, k1.
- Keeping first and last st of every row in St st, work even through Row 8 (10, 12, 14) if working from written st pattern, or through Row 14 if working from chart.

SHAPE SLEEVE

- *Inc Row (RS):* Continuing to work first and last st in St st, change to Rev St st across rem sts. Inc 2 sts this row, then every 2 (4, 6, 6) rows 4 more times, as follows: K1, p1, M1PL, purl to last 2 sts, M1PR, p1, k1—31 (35, 39, 43) sts.
- Work even until piece measures 5 (7, 9, 9½)" [12.5 (18, 23, 24) cm], ending with a WS row.

BODY

- *Next Row (RS):* CO 11 (15, 19, 23) sts using backwards loop method, k1, purl to end—42 (50, 58, 66) sts.
- *Next Row:* CO 11 (15, 19, 23) sts using backwards loop method, p1, knit to last st, p1—53 (65, 77, 89) sts.
- Keeping first and last st of every row in St st, work even for 3 (3½, 4, 4½)" from CO for body, ending with a WS row.
- *Next Row (RS):* Work Rows 1–12 of Edging Pattern across all sts.**
- *Next Row (RS):* Bind off 27 (33, 39, 45) sts in pattern. Transfer rem 26 (32, 38, 44) sts to a holder; set aside.

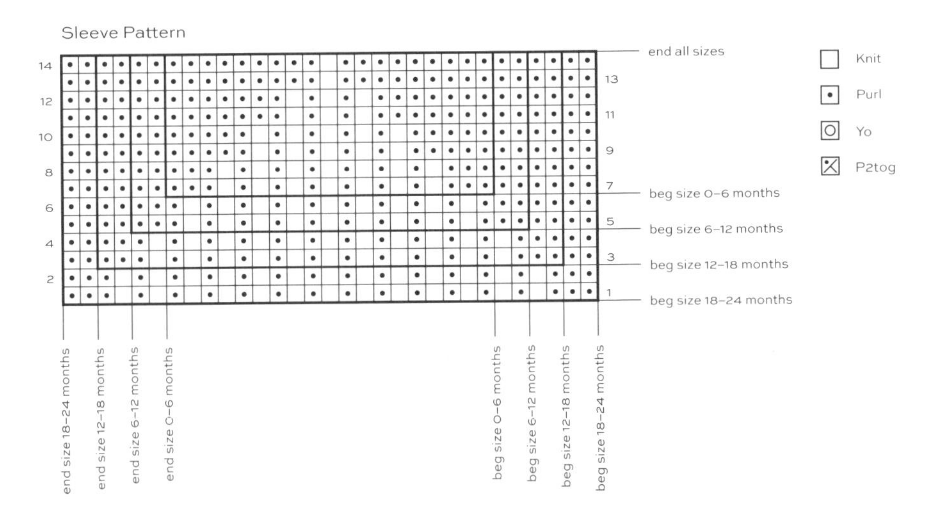

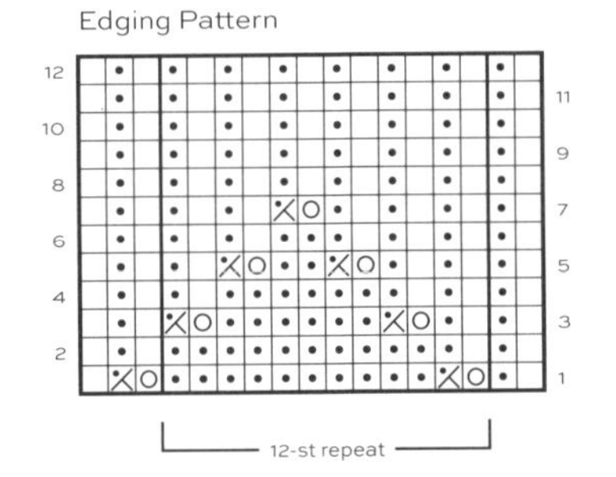

The two halves are attached at the center back with a 3-needle bind-off; the seam becomes a design element on the public side.

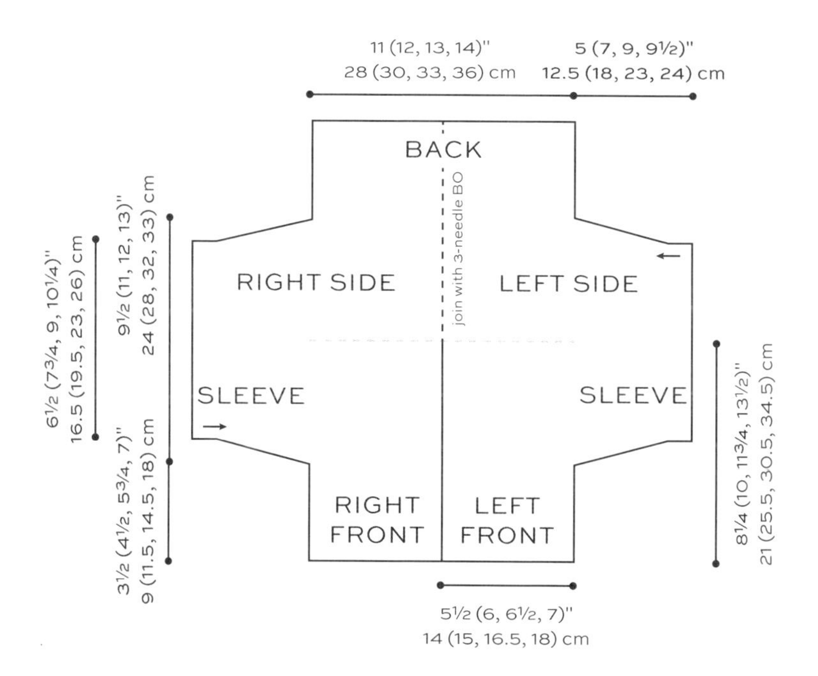

LEFT SIDE

Work as for Right Side to **.

FINISHING

Return held Right Side sts to a spare needle, and join Right and Left Sides using 3-needle BO, as follows: Hold the Sides with the WSs facing each other and the needles parallel. Using third needle and always working first st on front needle tog with first st on back needle, k2tog, *k2tog, pass first st over second st to BO 1 st; rep from * until all Right Side sts are BO, then BO rem 27 (33, 39, 45) Left Side sts in pattern. Sew side and sleeve seams.

FRONT TIES

Measure approx 3 (4, 5, 6)" [7.5 (10, 12.5, 15) cm] up from lower front edge. Using crochet hook, join yarn with a slip st to base of deepest rib within Edging Pattern and crochet firm chain 8" long. Fasten off. Rep for opposite front edge.

Cockleshell Cardigan in Light Lac & Iron, and yarn balls in (clockwise from top): Osage & Iron, Madder Root, Ice, Rust, Udo, Flamingo, and Light Lac & Iron.

SHAKERAG TOP

Design by

Amy Christoffers

As we shed the layers of winter, we crave light, warmth, air. Here, we applaud Amy Christoffers's sophisticated understanding of the nature of knitted fabrics.

It's a striped fabric made from exactly one yarn. The subtlety and cleverness of this is something we really love. Using two strands of Jade Sapphire Sylph, we make the stripes first with one strand, then two strands carried together.

Sylph is a rare, dreamy blend of cashmere and linen, really special.

The shape is as elemental as imaginable—it is worked from the bottom up, in the round, until dividing to work the top part back and forth. There is plenty of ease in this pullover, and drape.

The result is such that you'll be constantly holding up your fabric to admire the effect of a beautiful yarn worked in such a surprisingly simple way.

FINISHED MEASUREMENTS

Bust: 39 (44, 48, 53, 57½, 62½)"
[99 (112, 122, 134.5, 146, 159) cm]
Length: 22 (22, 22½, 23, 23½, 24)"
[56 (56, 57, 58.5, 59.5, 61) cm]

SIZES

To fit S (M, L, XL, 2XL, 3XL)
Note: This garment was designed with approx 4–8" (10–20.5 cm) of ease. Please take this into consideration when selecting your size.

MATERIALS

- Sylph by Jade Sapphire [50 g skeins, each approx 309 yds (202 m), 58% cashmere/42% linen]: 4 (4, 4, 5, 5, 6) skeins Hush, Eucalyptus, Maidenhair, or Loam
- Size US 4 (3.5 mm) circular needles, 16" (40 cm) and 32" (80 cm) long
- Size US 6 (4 mm) circular needle, 32" (80 cm) long, or size needed to achieve gauge
- Stitch markers
- Stitch holder

GAUGE

20 sts and 26 rows = 4" (10 cm) over St st, using larger needles and 2 strands of yarn held together

STRIPE SEQUENCE

Working in St st, *work 6 rnds/rows using 1 strand of yarn, then work 6 rnds/rows using 2 strands of yarn held tog; rep from * for Stripe Sequence.
Note: When working with 1 strand only, carry strand not in use up WS (up outside edge if working in rows), twisting strands at beginning of rnd to prevent a hole.

NOTE

Body is worked in the round to the end of the underarm shaping, then Back and Front are worked separately in rows to the shoulders.

BODY

- With 2 strands of yarn held tog, using 32" (80 cm) long smaller needle, CO 196 (220, 240, 264, 288, 312) sts. Join, being careful not to twist sts; pm for beg of rnd and work in the rnd as follows:
- Purl 1 rnd, [knit 1 rnd, purl 1 rnd] twice.
- Change to larger needle and begin Stripe Sequence; work even until piece measures 12" (30.5 cm).
- *Next Rnd:* K98 (110, 120, 132, 144, 156), pm, knit to end.

SHAPE UNDERARMS

- *Inc Row (RS):* Continuing in Stripe Sequence, inc 4 sts this rnd, then every other rnd 5 more times, as follows: [K1, M1R, knit to 1 st before marker, M1L, k1, sm] twice—220 (244, 264, 288, 312, 336) sts; 110 (122, 132, 144, 156, 168) sts each for front and back.

DIVIDE FOR FRONT AND BACK

- *Next Row (RS):* Knit to marker and place last 110 (122, 132, 144, 156, 168) sts worked on holder for front; knit to end—110 (122, 132, 144, 156, 168) sts rem for back.

BACK

- Working on back sts only, work even until armhole measures 6 (6, 6½, 7, 7½, 8)" [15 (15, 16.5, 18, 19, 20.5) cm], ending with a RS row.
- *Next Row (WS):* P31 (37, 42, 48, 54, 60), pm, p48, pm, purl to end.

SHAPE SHOULDERS AND NECK

NOTE: *Shoulders and neck are shaped at the same time; please read entire section through before beg.*

- *Next Row (RS):* BO 4 (4, 5, 7, 7, 9) sts at beg of next 14 (2, 6, 6, 10, 2) rows, then 0 (5, 6, 6, 8, 8) sts at beg of next 0 (12, 8, 8, 4, 12) rows. AT THE SAME TIME, beg on 7th row of shoulder shaping, shape neck as follows:
- *Next Row (RS):* Continuing to work shoulder shaping as established, work across to marker, join second ball of yarn, BO center 48 sts, knit to end.
- Working both sides at the same time, BO 1 st at each neck edge 3 times.

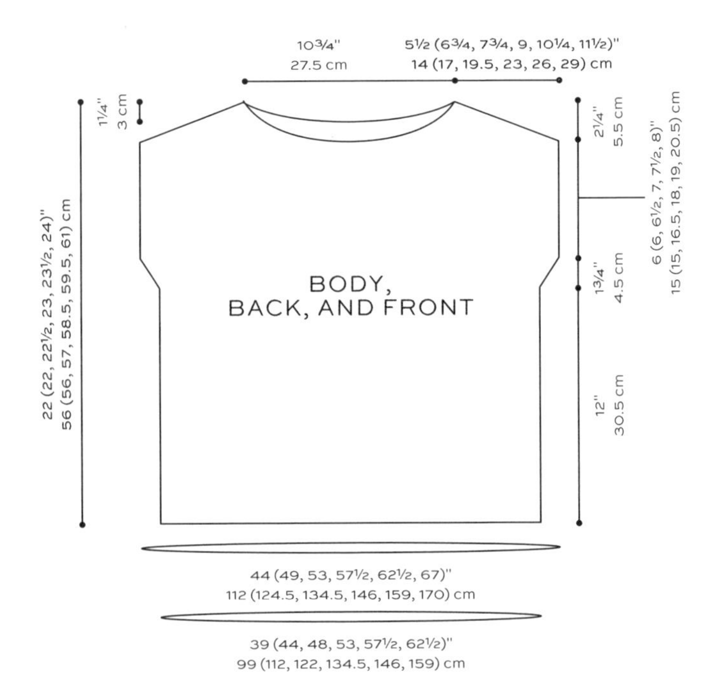

FRONT

— Transfer front sts to larger needle. With WS facing, rejoin yarn to front and work even until armhole measures 6 (6, 6½, 7, 7½, 8)" [15 (15, 16.5, 18, 19, 20.5) cm], ending with a RS row.

— *Next Row (WS):* P36 (42, 47, 53, 59, 65), pm, p38, pm, purl to end.

SHAPE SHOULDERS/NECK

NOTE: *Shoulders/neck are shaped at same time; read instructions to end before beg.*

Next Row (RS): BO 4 (4, 5, 7, 7, 9) sts, work across to marker, join second ball of yarn, BO center 38 sts, knit to end. Working both sides at the same time, BO 4 (4, 5, 7, 7, 9) sts at beg of next 13 (1, 5, 5, 9, 1) row(s), then 0 (5, 6, 6, 8, 8) sts at beg of next 0 (12, 8, 8, 4, 12) rows. AT THE SAME TIME, BO 2 sts at each neck edge twice, then 1 st at each neck edge 4 times.

FINISHING

Sew shoulder seams.

NECKBAND

With RS facing, using 16" (40 cm) long needle and 2 strands of yarn held tog, and beg at left shoulder seam, pick up and knit 10 sts along left front neck edge, 38 sts in center front BO sts, 10 sts to shoulder, 5 sts along right back neck edge, 48 sts in center back BO sts, and 5 sts to shoulder—116 sts.

NOTE: *The exact st count is not critical.*

BO off all sts knitwise.

ARMHOLE EDGING

With RS facing, using 16" (40 cm) long needle and 2 strands of yarn held tog, and beg at underarm, pick up and knit approx 66 (66, 72, 78, 84, 90) sts around armhole edge, picking up at a rate of approx 3 sts for every 4 rows.

NOTE: *The exact st count is not critical.*

BO all sts knitwise.

Weave in ends and block as desired.

Shakerag Top swatches in (top to bottom): Maidenhair, Loam, and Eucalyptus.

VISIBLE MENDING

A COUPLE OF YEARS AGO, I BEGAN TO SEE something intriguing in my Instagram feed. The hashtag—#visiblemending.

I was raised with the idea that mending is a thing to be done as invisibly as possible. A good mend passed without notice. In my mom's and grandmothers' days, mended clothing was a sign of poverty. Being frugal by necessity was nothing to be ashamed of, but it was not information people wanted to broadcast to others via obvious patching and darning.

In elementary school, the only visible mending I knew of were iron-on patches for boys' jeans and corduroys. Girls were trained to sit quietly in clean, hole-free dresses and tights, not to rip their jeans, if they were lucky enough to have jeans. (All this was to change very rapidly in the 1970s, when we wore exuberantly patched and embellished wide-leg bell bottoms, un-picked the hems, and let the frayed edges drag on the ground. My mom, horrified, said, "I'm glad your Aunt Carrie didn't live to see this.")

Tif Fussell's overalls.

Today, visible mending has taken root and flourished in the online maker movement. My Instagram feed is filled with beautiful examples of artful patches, darns, and reweavings, each showing where something has been broken, and then mended, with frankness and even pride.

Tom Van Deijnen (@TomofHolland) gives workshops in which he teaches techniques revived from antique mending samplers and books, from a time when mending was a survival skill. His mended blankets not only save damaged woven cloth from the landfill, but command prices reflecting fine workmanship.

Katrina Rodabaugh's (@katrinarodabaugh) Japanese sashiko-influenced mends give mass-produced jeans individual verve and personality.

And Tif Fussell (@dottieangel) combines her artful mending with handmade embellishments in wool and cloth, for rich results on clothing and homewares.

These talented artisans and other visible menders have managed to create a shift in how we perceive mending. Extending the life of textiles now is not only respectable, it's something we want to be seen. Where the women who raised me would have cringed, I can only look on with curiosity and fascination, and an eagerness to give it a try myself.

— Kay

PEEK-THROUGH COWL/SCARF

Design by

Amy Christoffers

WHEN WE KNIT LACE IN THIN, FILMY mohair yarn, we achieve maximum transparency. The method—full of peepholes—and the barely-there material combine to let as much light through as possible.

We have long been fascinated with layered lace. Apart from the sheerness, the weightless texture is beguiling. When Amy showed us a swatch in which two yarns continually combined and separated, creating columns of transparency against a marled garter background, we only had one question: Can we do it in Loft, a laceweight mohair/silk blend hand-dyed by Karida Collins? The exquisite swatches that came back answered with a resounding yes.

We show two cowls here (and a third on page 29). To make a scarf, you simply follow the pattern as written, but skip the finishing step when the two ends are seamed together.

NOTES

The entire piece is worked using both A and B on each row; you begin with 1 strand each of A and B held together, then alternate working with each color separately, then with both colors together again.

The single-color sections are worked in double knitting. Each color in these sections is worked separately, resulting in a double layer of fabric. The color not in use is "dropped" (left out of work) to the front or back of the work as indicated in the instructions. Pay close attention to where you are instructed to leave the yarn that is not in use—whether to the front or to the back—as this will ensure that the colors remain separate for the sections that are worked separately. Leave the color not in work in place where you dropped it while you work with the other color.

The color you're knitting with in single-color sections is always held to the front when not in work; the color you're purling with in single-color sections is always held to the back when not in work. Be careful not to twist the yarns together when switching sides in between the single colors. You may find it helpful to check your work after each row to make sure that the single-color sections stay separate, and that you don't have errant opposite-color floats in front of the work on either side.

When going from single-color to 2-strand sections, pull the yarn a bit more tightly when you work the first st.

There is no RS or WS to this piece, but to help you keep track of your work, odd-numbered rows (where A is the dominant color) will be labeled as RS rows.

If you don't have experience knitting with laceweight mohair, allow yourself some time to acclimate to its tendency to float around and also to stick to itself. Once you've done the fiddling required to set up that first row, work slowly and be patient as you settle into your preferred way of keeping the two strands separate when they need to be separate, and together when they need to be together. Once you stop fighting the yarn (or it stops fighting you), you will find a rhythm and amaze onlookers, whether they knit or not.

For variation, instead of the recommended US size 8 needle, try a US size 10½. Guess what happens? (Hint: even more light, even less weight.)

KNITTED MEASUREMENTS

Width: Approx 8" (20.5 cm)

Cowl Circumference: Approx 48" (122 cm)

Scarf Length: Approx 56" (142 cm)

MATERIALS

- Neighborhood Fiber Co. Loft [1 oz skeins, each approx 350 yds (320 m), 60% kid mohair/40% silk]:

  Gray/Green

  A: Thomas Circle, 1 skein

  B: Belair, 1 skein

  Purple/Pink

  A: Shaw, 1 skein

  B: Victorian Village, 1 skein

  Gray/Pink

  A: Gwynn Oak, 1 skein

  B: Charles Centre, 1 skein
- Size US 8 (5 mm) needles, or size needed to achieve open, airy fabric
- One double-pointed needle one size larger than main needle

GAUGE

Note: Gauge is not critical for this project. The goal is to achieve an open, airy fabric.

COWL/SCARF

Important: Read notes at left before you start knitting.

- Using 1 strand of A and B held together, CO 33 sts.
- *Set-Up Row (WS):* *With A and B held tog, k3, drop yarns with B to front and A to back and leave them there; without working the sts, split each of the next 3-st pairs into 2 separate sts, placing B sts on right needle and A sts on dpn (you now have 6 separate sts instead of 3 pair); slip the 3 A sts back to left needle, then slip the 3 B sts back to left needle in front of the A sts;
  with B (keeping A in back), k3, drop B to front;
  with A (keeping B in front), p3; rep from * to last 3 sts; with A and B held tog, k3—48 sts.

- *Row 1 (RS):* *With A and B held tog, k3, drop B to back and leave it there; with A, yo, sk2p, yrn, drop A to front and leave it there;
  with B, p3; rep from * to last 3 sts; with A and B held tog, k3.
- *Row 2:* *With A and B held tog, k3, drop A to back and leave it there; with B, k3, drop B to front and leave it there;
  with A, p3; rep from * to last 3 sts; with A and B held tog, k3.
- *Row 3:* *With A and B held tog, k3, drop B to back;
  with A, k3, drop A to front;
  with B, p3; rep from * to last 3 sts; with A and B held tog, k3.
- *Row 4:* *With A and B held tog, k3, drop A to back;
  with B, yo, sk2p, yrn, drop B to front;
  with A, p3; rep from * to last 3 sts; with A and B held tog, k3.
- *Row 5:* Rep Row 3.
  with A, k3, drop A to front;
  with B, p3; rep from * to last 3 sts; with A and B held tog, k3.
- *Row 6:* *With A and B held tog, k3, drop A to back;
  with B, k3, drop B to front;
  with A, p3; rep from * to last 3 sts; with A and B held tog, k3.
- Rep Rows 1–6 until piece measures 48" (122 cm) for cowl or 56" (142 cm) for scarf or to desired length (leaving enough yarn for BO row and to sew ends tog if working the cowl), ending with Row 6.
- *BO Row:* With A and B held tog, BO 2 sts; *slip 3 sts to right needle, then 3 sts to dpn, [slip 1 st from right needle back to left needle, then slip 1 st from dpn back to left needle] 3 times; with A and B held tog, knitting 1 st of each color tog as you BO, BO next six 2-st pairs; rep from * to end. Fasten off rem st.

FINISHING

Cowl: Sew CO and BO edges tog.
Cowl and Scarf: Weave in ends, block as desired.

We experimented with four and five cables for our cowls. The pattern is written for five. If you want to omit one, cast on 27 stitches instead of 33.

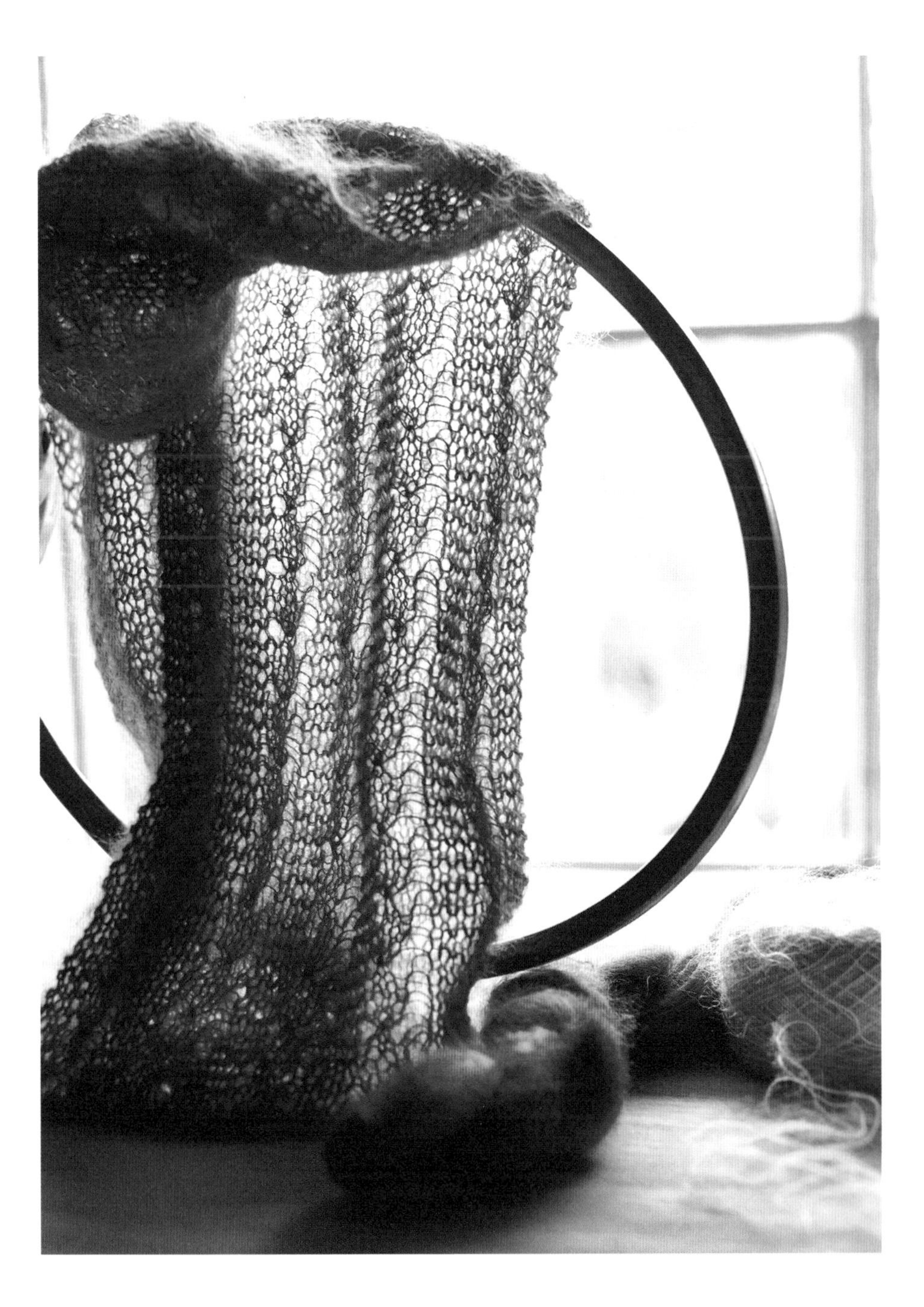

THE PARADOX *of* LACE

LACE IS NOT NECESSARY. IT'S EXTRA. It's the edge of a pillowcase, a veil worn once, the fillip and flair on a fancy handkerchief.

We measure time by the things we make, and with lace, this distillation of patience and pattern and time and toil results in this most extraordinary thing.

Lace concentrates a maker's time like little else. It requires patience, focus, and trust—trust that this enormous amount of work spent on a shapeless mass of threads or yarn will end in a glorious thing that's barely there.

Almost invisible, yet most decidedly there, lace dazzles us with the extravagance of work in such a concentrated form. It's a princess dress, a baby gown, a stone from the sea with a covering of crochet. Lace leaves behind the everyday. And maybe that's why we treasure it so.

—Ann

Lace-covered stones by Margaret Glinski-Oomen.

ALBERS SHAWL

Design by

Amy Christoffers

CONFESSION: WE WILL KNIT ANYTHING that claims to be inspired by the work of Anni Albers, the multi-disciplinary artist best remembered for her textile designs. Albers's weaving, by hand or machine, often had geometric and organic qualities, and her choice of materials was unorthodox. One of Albers's early designs at the Bauhaus school was a wall covering woven from cotton, chenille, and cellophane that reflected light while absorbing sound.

Inspired by Albers, Amy Christoffers plays with the transmission of light in this shawl. The background colors—worked in crisp linen—are consistent throughout the design, and the "windows" of color—worked in a tweedy silk, merino, cashmere blend—are made by simply adding another strand and knitting it together with the background color. It's like intarsia without worrying about gaps at color change junctions. It's a simple and liberating way to play with color and see one color "through" another.

KNITTED MEASUREMENTS

16" × 60" (40.5 × 152.5 cm)

MATERIALS

- Reed by Shibui Knits [50 g skeins, each approx 246 yds (225 m), 100% linen]
- Pebble by Shibui Knits [25 gram skeins, each approx 224 yds (205 m), 48% recycled silk/ 36% fine merino/16% cashmere]
  Sample Colorway:
  A: Reed in Fog, 1 skein
  B: Pebble in Shore, 1 skein
  C: Reed in Caffeine, 1 skein
  D: Reed in Ash, 1 skein
- Size US 6 (4 mm) needles, or size needed to achieve gauge

GAUGE

20 sts and 33 rows = 4" (10 cm) over St st using 1 strand each of A and B held together

NOTE

When changing colors, twist new and old colors together once to prevent a hole.

SHAWL

- Using long-tail CO and A, CO 80 sts.
- Knit 1 row. Work in St st, beg with a RS row, until piece measures 3" (7.5 cm), ending with a WS row.
- *Row 1 (RS):* With A, k40; join B and with 1 strand each of A and B held tog, k25, drop B to back; with A, knit to end.
- *Rows 2, 4, 6, 8, and 10:* With A, p15; with 1 strand each of A and B held tog, p25, drop B to front; with A, purl to end.
- *Rows 3, 5, 7, 9, and 11:* Rep Row 1.
- *Row 12:* With A, p15; with 1 strand each of A and B held tog, p50, drop B to front; with A, purl to end.
- *Rows 13, 15, 17, 19, and 21:* With A, k15; with 1 strand each of A and B held tog, k25, drop B to back; with A, knit to end.
- *Rows 14, 16, 18, 20, and 22:* With A, p40; with 1 strand each of A and B held tog, p25, drop B to front; with A, purl to end.
- *Row 23:* With A, k15; with 1 strand each of A and B held tog, k50, drop B to back; with A, knit to end.
- Rep Rows 2–23 five more times. Cut A and join C.

- Using C in place of A, rep Rows 2–23 six more times. Cut C and join D.
- Using D in place of A, rep Rows 2–23 six more times.
- Cut B and work even with D for 3" (7.5 cm), ending with a RS row. BO all sts knitwise.
- Weave in ends. Wet block finished piece and pin to desired measurements.

The "wrong" side of this shawl is equally as show-worthy as the "right" side.

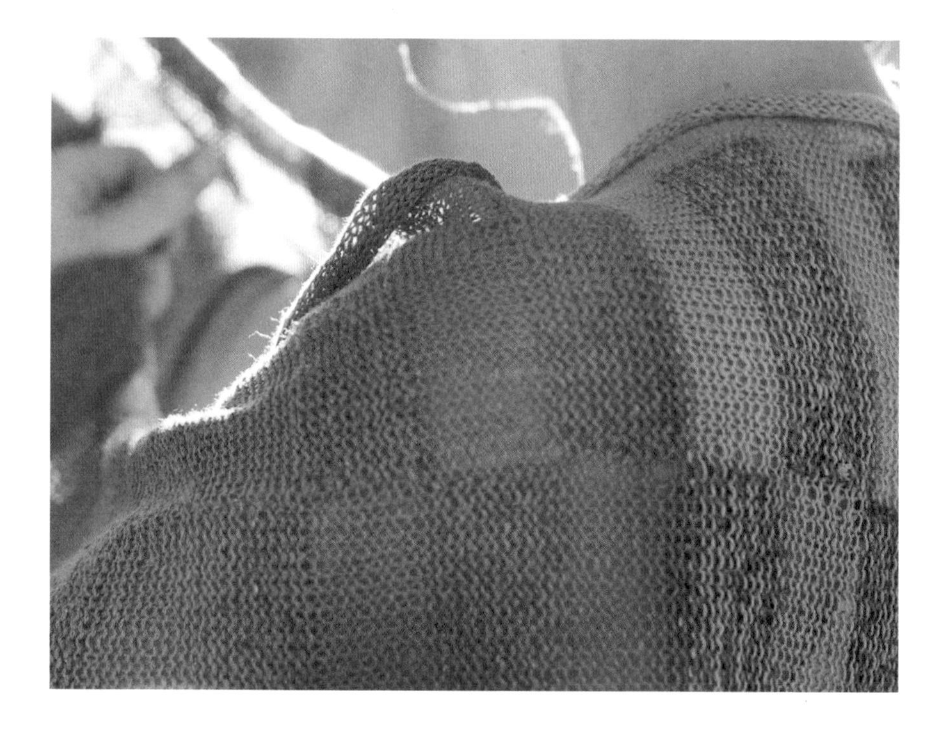

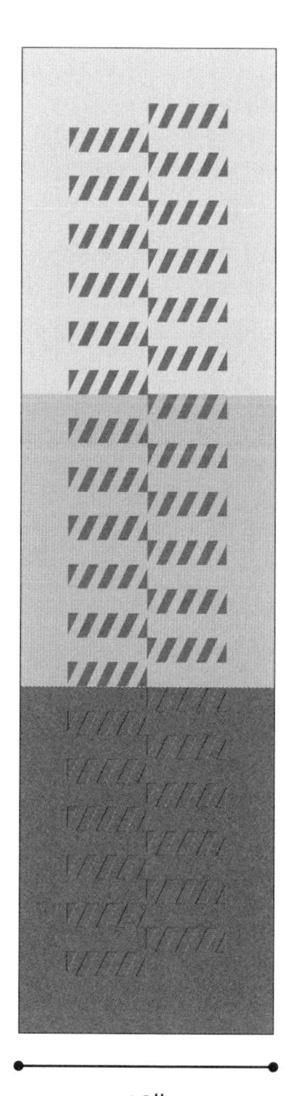

A

B

C

D

1 strand each of A and B held tog

1 strand each of B and C held tog

1 strand each of B and D held tog

ALBERS IMPROVISATION: PLAYING WITH STRIPES, TRANSPARENCY, AND OPACITY

As Amy began mocking up sketches for the opaque shapes in the Albers Shawl, she couldn't stop coming up with variations on the theme. Ultimately, she settled on a simple repetition of shifting stripes of opaque fabric in a transparent background, but she hopes (as do we) that her design will serve as a jumping-off point for lots of creative play.

In order to keep the method of working simple, just a few rules: Begin with a ground of one yarn and introduce the second yarn by holding the two yarns together for sections. In the interest of not having too many ends to weave in, keep the sections connected at one point or another. That's it.

Follow your intuition: Do you want your shapes to shift subtly or take up big blocks of space? Do you like the idea of skinny stripes worked throughout like an open sky streaked with clouds? Or random stripes at irregular intervals like a cityscape? Perhaps your shapes should follow the rhythm of a favorite piece of music. You might want to start with just one background color and one contrast color, then as you get your groove going, add more complexity. Shown here are a couple of illustrations to get you started.

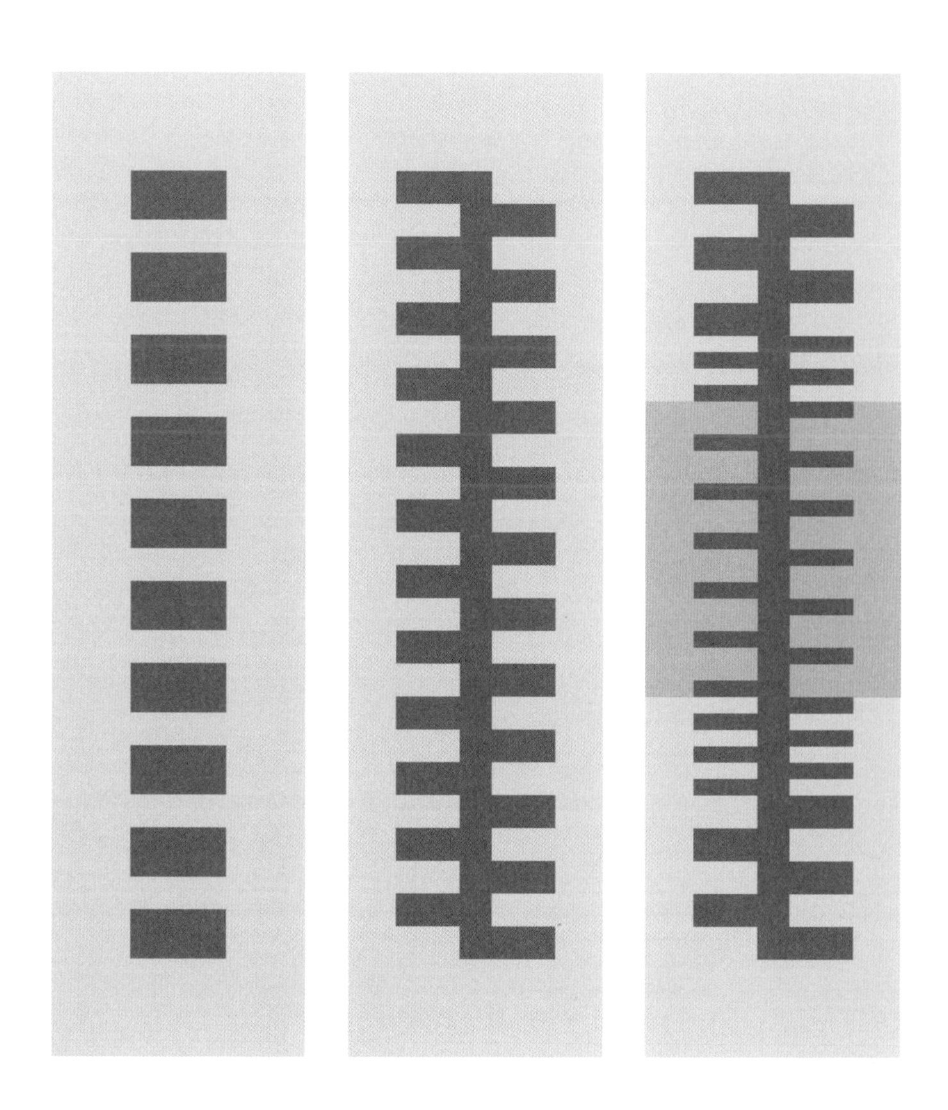

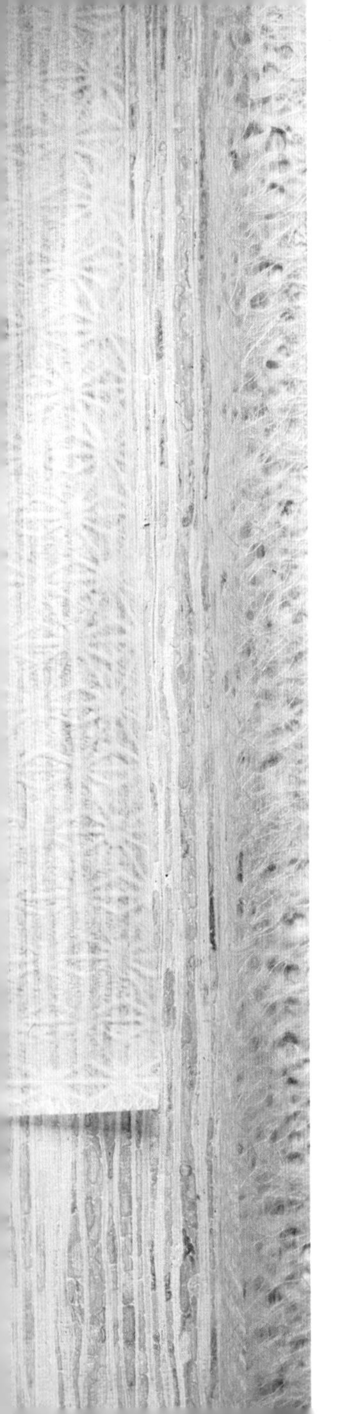

GETTING TO KNOW AMY CHRISTOFFERS

Amy Christoffers is the creator of the Savory Knitting line of patterns as well as the design director at Berroco Yarns. She is the author of the book *New American Knits*, and her work can also be seen in *Pom Pom Quarterly*, *Making*, *Amirisu*, Brooklyn Tweed's *Wool People*, *Interweave Knits*, and *Twist Collective*. She lives in a tiny house in the mountains of Vermont with her husband and son.

When did you know you wanted to be a designer?

As a very little girl I remember taping together my grandmother's quilting scraps to make Barbie ball gowns and then cutting up pillowcases to make dresses for myself, so my interest in designing clothing has been nearly lifelong. I got my first sewing machine when I was 8 and continued making my own clothes through high school, though I have to admit I was never very good at it. I studied fine art at Montserrat College of Art in Massachusetts and taught myself to knit because I couldn't fit a sewing machine into my tiny apartment. The knitting soon took over everything, and I spent the next decade trying to learn every single thing about it.

How did you go about learning?

I mainly learned from books. While I was in college, which was in the late 1990s, I read the ones I could find at the public library, which were from the 1970s and 1980s and filled with intarsia sweater vests, knitted lace wrap dresses, and Brady Bunch families in matching ski hats and scarves. Then I spent a long time swatching stitch patterns from Lesley Stanfield's *The New Knitting Stitch Library* and *Knitting Counterpanes* by Mary Walker Phillips. The two publications that inspired me to learn how to follow a pattern were the Summer 2000 issue of *Interweave Knits*, which was filled with modern designs based on traditional/regional knitting styles, and the 2001 Rowan collection called *A Season's Tale*.

How did you make the leap to becoming a knitwear designer?

I didn't even realize being a knitwear designer could be a way to make a living until I read Melanie Falick's book *Knitting in America*. It took me nearly 10 years to build up the skill and courage to submit my ideas to editors. My first published design was a cardigan in *Interweave Knits* in 2010.

What does your ideal design process look like today?

I still love to swatch. When possible, I like to swatch a yarn over and over until it tells me what it wants to be, which can be very time-consuming. Once I have an idea of what I want to make, I enjoy plotting it out on paper; it's like solving a puzzle. I make schematics that look a lot like Japanese knitting patterns before I write out instructions in words.

Aside from knitting, what are some of the other creative pursuits you enjoy spending time on?

I struggle because my desire to learn new hobbies and crafts is at odds with my responsibilities and obligations. I get excited and inspired and I want to make and do it all! There are two constants, however: Sewing is always going to be my first love though I'm not very good at it and find it to be very humbling. Cooking is my daily meditation. I am addicted to the *New York Times* Cooking app, and I collect cookbooks. My favorites are the big technique-filled classics with words like *Mastering*, *Art of* and *Essential* in the titles. For a while I was baking bread, and for a couple of summers I was pickle and preserve crazy, but what I love most is making dinner every night. I can try things and who cares if one dinner fails? I'll try something else tomorrow.

ABBREVIATIONS

Beg: Begin(ning)(s)

BO: Bind off

Cn: Cable needle

CO: Cast on

Dpn: Double-pointed needle(s)

Inc: Increas(ed)(es)(ing)

M1L: (make 1 left) Insert left needle front to back under horizontal strand between stitch just worked and next stitch on left needle. Knit this strand through back loop. 1 stitch increased.

M1PL: (make 1 purlwise, left) Insert left needle front to back under horizontal strand between stitch just worked and next stitch on left needle. Purl this strand through back loop. 1 stitch increased.

M1PR: (make 1 purlwise, right) Insert left needle back to front under horizontal strand between stitch just worked and next stitch on left needle. Purl this strand through front loop. 1 stitch increased.

M1R: (make 1 right) Insert left needle back to front under horizontal strand between stitch just worked and next stitch on left needle. Knit this strand through front loop. 1 stitch increased.

P2tog: Purl 2 stitches together.

Pm: Place marker

Rep: Repeat(ed)(ing)(s)

Rev St st: reverse Stockinette stitch

Rnd(s): Round(s)

RS: Right side

Sk2p: Slip next stitch to right needle knitwise, knit 2 together, pass slipped stitch over. 2 stitches decreased.

Sm: Slip marker

St st: Stockinette stitch

St(s): Stitch(es)

Tog: Together

WS: Wrong side

Yo: Yarn over

Yrn: (yarn round needle) Bring yarn under needle to front of work, over needle to back, then under needle to front again, creating a stitch on needle.

A WHO'S WHO

This MDK Field Guide *marks our sixth little book exploring the big world of knitting. In each Field Guide we feature patterns from clever designers who think about knitting in inspiring ways.*

NO. 1: STRIPES
Mary Jane Mucklestone,
Antonia Shankland,
Ann Weaver

NO. 2: FAIR ISLE
Véronik Avery, Ann Budd,
Michèle Rose Orne

NO. 3: WILD YARNS
Kirstin Kapur, Sue McCain,
Dianna Walla

NO. 4: LOG CABIN
Ann Weaver,
Kay Gardiner

NO. 5: SEQUENCES
Cecelia Campochiaro

We work with the most distinctive yarn makers to create kits to go with all the patterns in the *MDK Field Guides*. These kits are available, often in limited editions and unique colorways made just for us, at MasonDixonKnitting.com/shop.

Berroco
Blue Sky Fibers
Brooklyn Tweed
Brown Sheep Company
Canon Hand Dyes
Crave Yarn
Freia Fine Handpaints
Hazel Knits
Jade Sapphire
Jill Draper Makes Stuff
Lichen and Lace
Neighborhood Fiber Co.
Nutmeg Fibers
Rowan
Shibui Knits
Sincere Sheep
Spincycle Yarns
Swans Island